The
Puzzle of the Dinosaur-Bird

THE STORY OF *ARCHAEOPTERYX*

MIRIAM SCHLEIN

Pictures by MARK HALLETT

Dial Books for Young Readers New York

Published by Dial Books for Young Readers
A Division of Penguin Books USA Inc.
375 Hudson Street
New York, New York 10014

Designed by Nancy R. Leo
Printed in Hong Kong
First Edition
1 3 5 7 9 10 8 6 4 2

Library of Congress Cataloging in Publication Data
Schlein, Miriam.
The puzzle of the dinosaur-bird: the story of Archaeopteryx
by Miriam Schlein; illustrated by Mark Hallett. —1st ed.
p.   cm.
ISBN 0-8037-1282-0.—ISBN 0-8037-1283-9 (lib. bdg.)
1. Archaeopteryx—Juvenile literature. [1. Archaeopteryx. 2. Dinosaurs.]
I. Hallett, Mark, 1947– ill. II. Title.
QE872.A8S35 1996   568'.22—dc20   93-44586   CIP   AC

Special thanks to Dr. John Ostrom, Yale University,
for checking the facts in this book.

Mark Hallett's paintings are rendered in gouache.

To my mother, Joan, with love —M.H.

A Strange Discovery

In 1861 some men working in a limestone quarry in Germany found a really odd fossil. There, stuck in the limestone, was something that looked like a small dinosaur with feathers! The feathers themselves had long since decayed. But their outline could be clearly seen in the stone.

Only birds have feathers. That is our definition of a bird: an animal with feathers.

But this skeleton looked more like a dinosaur. It had a long bony tail like a dinosaur. Birds have a short stump of a tailbone. (A bird's tail may *look* long—but it's made of feathers, not bone.)

Its front limbs had claws. A bird's front limbs are wings. They don't have claws. And it had sharp little teeth. Birds don't have any teeth.

So—what was it? A bird? Or a dinosaur? It was a real puzzle. If it *was* a bird, it would be the oldest one ever found.

A German scientist named it *Archaeopteryx lithographica,* which means "ancient wing from lithographic limestone."

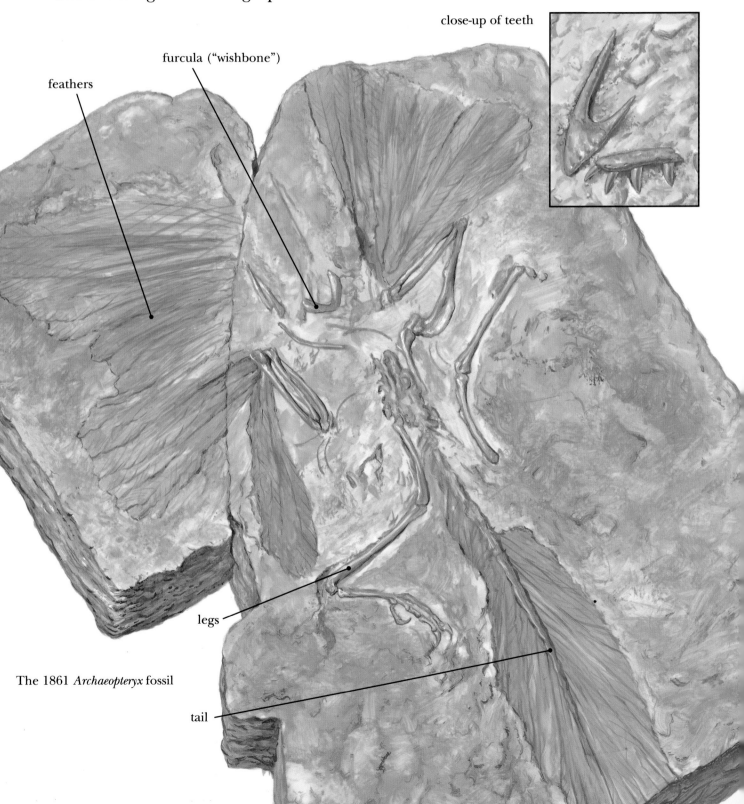

close-up of teeth

feathers

furcula ("wishbone")

legs

The 1861 *Archaeopteryx* fossil

tail

The fossil was sent to the British Museum, where it was examined by dinosaur expert Richard Owen. He was the man who had made up the word "dinosaur" just twenty years before. If anyone could figure out what the fossil was, he could.

Right away he could see the dinosaur features: the long tailbone, the front claws, the teeth found in part of a jawbone.

Of course he also saw the imprint of the feathers. And he saw another bird feature that was not so obvious: The fossil had a *furcula*. This is the bone we call the "wishbone." It is a special bone that only birds have. It is made up of right and left collarbones that are fused together. What it does is help to brace a bird's wings against wind pressure.

Richard Owen examined the fossil carefully for about a month. Then he announced his decision. *Archaeopteryx,* he said, was a bird. With feathers and a furcula, what else could it be?

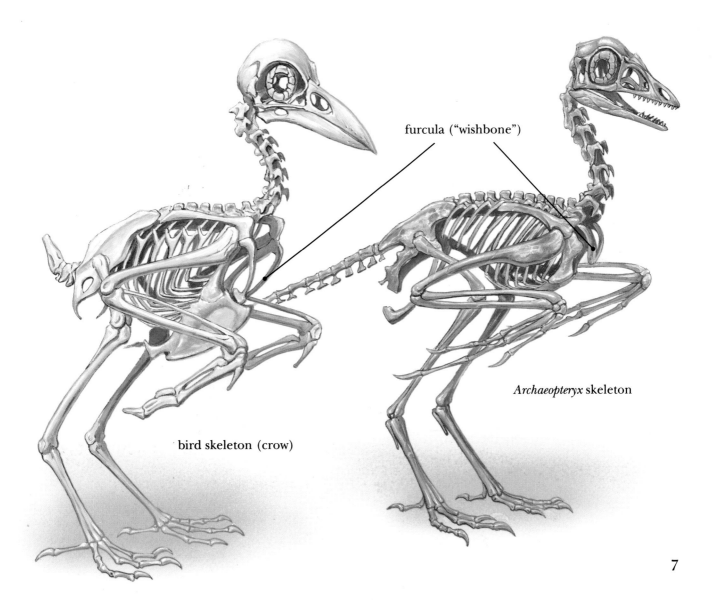

furcula ("wishbone")

Archaeopteryx skeleton

bird skeleton (crow)

The World of *Archaeopteryx*

Close your eyes. Imagine yourself in the world of *Archaeopteryx*. It's about 150 million years ago—the time we call the Jurassic Period. Skin-winged pterodactyls swoop about over a big, saltwater lagoon. Far out, some ichthyosaurs swim swiftly through the water. *Goniopholis,* a crocodile, is snoozing along the shore. A small dinosaur called *Compsognathus* is eating a lizard.

You might see a scrawny, furry, long-nosed little creature about the size of a squirrel. It is *Triconodon*, one of the earliest mammals.

Now, if you look carefully, you can see *Archaeopteryx* hiding in the leafy bushes. It is small, not much bigger than a crow. Its head is just two inches long. Its whole body—including that long tail—measures only about fourteen inches.

It stretches out its feathery forearms. But can it fly?

Was *Archaeopteryx* a Good Flyer?

Most scientists do not think *Archaeopteryx lithographica* was a good flyer.
More likely, they say, it was able to glide through the air—maybe for
quite a long distance. But they doubt that it could move through the air
very well on its own power—which is what true flying is. (It's like the
difference between coasting on your bike, or actively pedaling to move
ahead.) They imagine it flapping along with great effort for a short
distance, then coming to a crash landing.

Many birds today are skilled flyers, able to fly thousands of miles, over mountains and oceans. Why couldn't *Archaeopteryx lithographica* do this? It had wings. It had feathers.

But the way its wings were attached to the shoulder did not seem to allow for a good flapping motion. Also, birds today have a strong breastbone. Their flying muscles are attached to it. *Archaeopteryx lithographica* did not seem to have a breastbone.

Gregory Paul is a scientist who has a different point of view. He is convinced that *Archaeopteryx lithographica* was a good "power-flyer."

True, it didn't seem to have that breastbone for flight muscle attachment. But it did seem to have strong wing bones. And there were signs that it had strong wing muscles. (You can see a long ridge on the wing bones where the muscles were attached.) And remember, *Archaeopteryx* did have a furcula—that special bone that helps birds to fly. Paul believes that the furcula could have supported muscles powerful enough for flying.

Gregory Paul, in fact, has a whole different picture of the *Archaeopteryx* way of life. He thinks *Archaeopteryx* was more than a good flyer. He thinks it was a good swimmer as well, and could "fly" through the water the way penguins do.

He imagines *Archaeopteryx* nesting in bushes, out on islands that dotted the great saltwater lagoon. He sees it swooping down, dive-bombing for fish like a fish hawk.

What gives him this idea? The clue, he says, is in the teeth. *Archaeopteryx* teeth had thick, barrel-shaped roots. Animals that eat fish often have this kind of teeth.

Archaeopteryx tooth

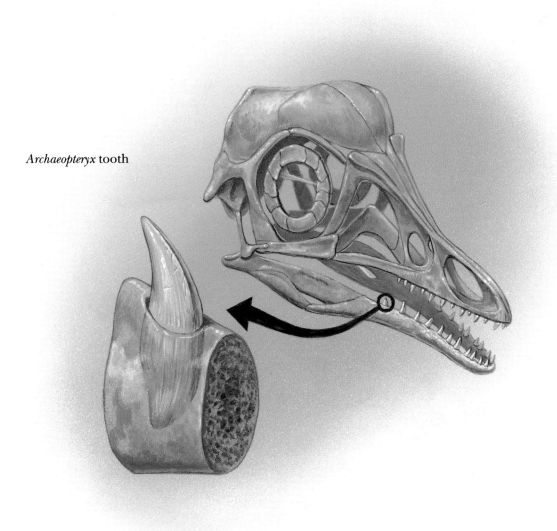

How Did *Archaeopteryx* Begin to Fly?

Some scientists think *Archaeopteryx* began flying *up* from a running start on the ground. It might have started by leaping up into a tree for safety. Or maybe it ran along, trying to catch insects in its feathery arms, and once in a while leaped up into the air to grab a flying insect. Or

perhaps, as it ran away from an enemy such as *Allosaurus,* a wind current gave it a lift and pushed it along, causing it to glide. It could have discovered that flapping its feathery arms up and down helped it to move farther and faster. And at some point it probably began to do more than gliding: It began to fly through the air on its own flapping power.

But most scientists do not agree. Why not? One reason, they say, is this: Its back claws were not worn down—as they would have been if *Archaeopteryx* did a lot of running.

Instead, they think it is more likely that *Archaeopteryx* began flying *down* from the trees. It could have started by jumping from one tree to another the way squirrels do, or by leaping down to the ground.

If it stretched its feathery arms out for balance, the wind might have pushed it into a glide, taking it farther than a plain jump. It might have discovered that moving its feathery arms up and down helped it to travel through the air even better. So maybe *Archaeopteryx* first started to fly this way—*down* from the trees, not *up* from the ground.

Ancestors of *Archaeopteryx*

Where did *Archaeopteryx* come from? Was it a descendant of the ptero-saurs?

No. Pterosaurs did not have feathers. Their wings, like bat wings, were made of skin. Pterosaurs, in fact, were not dinosaurs. They were flying reptiles. (Pterosaur means "wing reptile.")

HOW WERE DINOSAURS DIFFERENT FROM OTHER REPTILES?

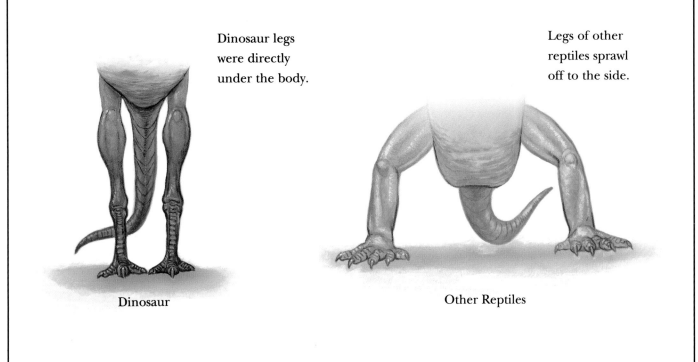

Dinosaur legs were directly under the body.

Legs of other reptiles sprawl off to the side.

Dinosaur

Other Reptiles

This was an important difference. It is what made dinosaurs able to become good walkers and runners.

Archaeopteryx probably developed from one of the small dinosaurs. In some ways it still was like a dinosaur. In other ways it was getting to be more like a bird. Its feathers probably developed from frayed scales.

Scientists sometimes call *Archaeopteryx* a "transitional bird" because it was in the process of changing from dinosaur to bird. To English scientist Thomas Huxley that was the most exciting thing about *Archae-opteryx.* A few years earlier, in 1859, Charles Darwin had come out with his astonishing new theory of evolution. It showed how a kind of living thing can evolve, or change over time, through many generations, into something quite different. And now, here was *Archaeopteryx*—a perfect example of this!

Archaeopteryx is often called the "missing link" between dinosaurs and birds. To Huxley it showed that birds are probably descended directly from the dinosaurs. He pointed out how dinosaurs and birds were alike:

- Their skeletons are similar in many details.
- Dinosaurs and birds both have a certain kind of ankle joint that no other kind of animal has.
- Dinosaur hip bones are often shaped like bird hips.
- Many dinosaurs have birdlike beaks.
- Many dinosaurs also have long, flexible, birdlike necks.
- Like birds, many dinosaurs have air spaces in their bones.
- Dinosaurs and birds lay eggs.

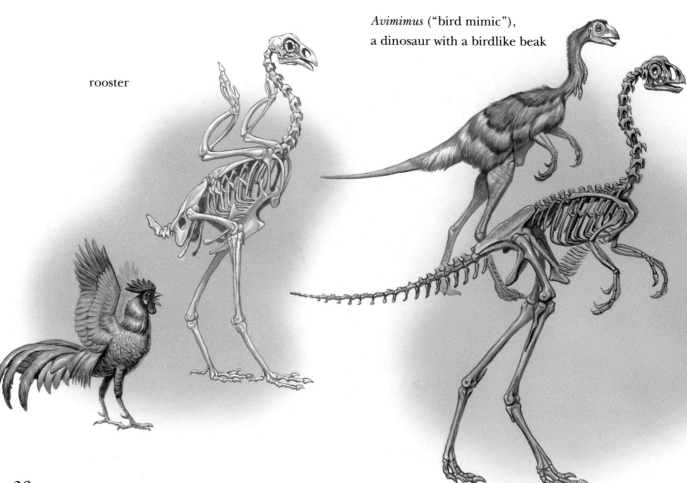

rooster

Avimimus ("bird mimic"), a dinosaur with a birdlike beak

20

- Dinosaur bodies are covered with scales. Birds' feet and legs have scales.
- Dinosaur feet are often shaped so much like birds' feet (three toes forward, one pointing back) that some dinosaur footprints were first thought to have been made by gigantic ancient birds.
- Like dinosaurs, *Archaeopteryx* had claws on its front limbs (its wings). Birds today do not have wing claws. But there is one South American bird, the hoatzin, that does have claws on its wings, for a short while, when it is young. It loses them as an adult.

Archaeopteryx

Juvenile (top)
and adult hoatzin
wings

For many years most scientists agreed with Huxley's idea that today's birds are direct descendants of the dinosaurs. Then, in the 1920s, a Danish scientist named Gerhard Heilmann came along and destroyed the whole theory. It wasn't possible, he said. Birds could not have stemmed directly from dinosaurs. Why not?

The reason he gave was this: That special bird bone, the furcula, is made of fused left and right collarbones. But dinosaurs did not have collarbones. So how could birds evolve from dinosaurs? Where would their furcula have come from?

Heilmann said that even though they were closely related, dinosaurs did not lead directly to birds. Instead, he believed that dinosaurs and

birds had a common ancestor—some early reptile. One possibility was *Euparkeria.*

Euparkeria was one of the pseudosuchians—"false crocodiles." Actually, it looked nothing like a crocodile. It was small and lively, and often ran about on its back legs. But most important—it had a collarbone. It all seemed to make sense. So, for the next fifty years or so, most paleontologists switched over to this idea.

Huxley's idea

Birds
↑
Dinosaurs

Heilmann's idea

Dinosaurs   Birds
↑   ↑
Euparkeria

Euparkeria chasing a dragonfly

A Case of Mistaken Identity

In 1970 paleontologist John Ostrom was in a museum in Holland, looking at a fossil labeled "Pterosaur." But to Ostrom it didn't look like a pterosaur. The feet and legs seemed too big. The fingers did not look right either. (The three smaller wing-fingers of a pterosaur are all the same length. These fingers were not.)

Dr. Ostrom became curious, and asked if he could take the fossil out of the case to get a better look at it. He took it to a good light and held it at an angle. What did he see? A faint outline of feathers! This was not a pterosaur at all. It was an *Archaeopteryx*. The fossil had been found in 1855, but had been wrongly identified for more than one hundred years. This discovery put John Ostrom right in the middle of the *Archaeopteryx* puzzle.

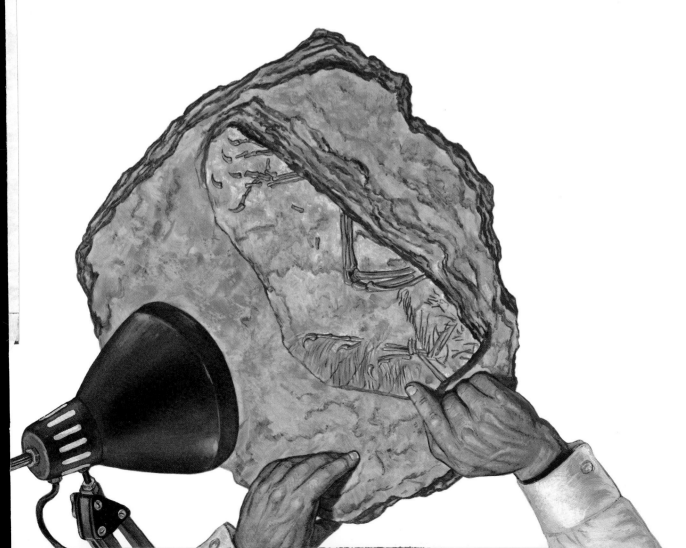

24

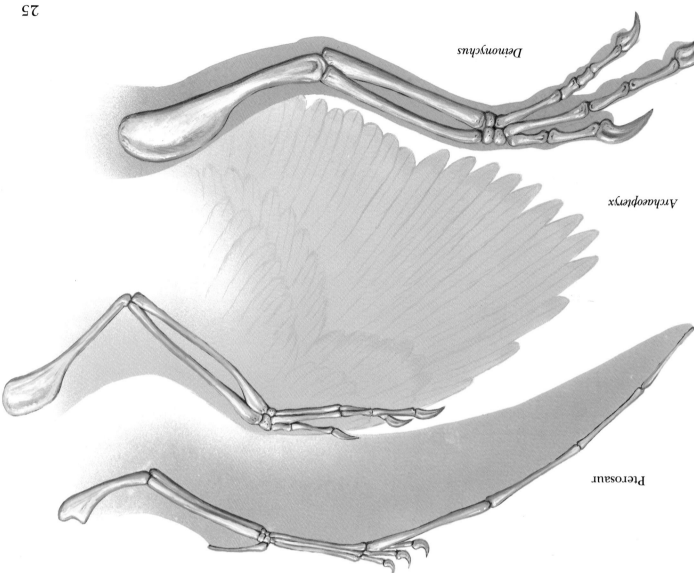

Deinonychus

Archaeopteryx

Pterosaur

Ostrom himself had just discovered a "new" dinosaur in Montana. It was a small, fierce flesh-eater with a big, hooked back claw, which it probably used to rip open its prey. He named it *Deinonychus*—"terrible claw."

When he examined *Archaeopteryx*, Ostrom was struck by something. Aside from its smaller size, and the fact that it did not have the "terrible claw," in many other ways—the fingers, the wrist bone, and the shape of the ankle, hip, and thigh—it looked a lot like *Deinonychus*.

Deinonychus was the kind of dinosaur we call a coelurosaur. Like birds, coelurosaurs had hollow spaces in their bones. (Coelurosaur means "hollow-tailed reptile.")

What did all this add up to? To John Ostrom it seemed to point to one thing. Thomas Huxley, back in the 1800s, had been right after all: Today's birds probably *are* direct descendants of some kind of dinosaur— most likely one of the coelurosaurs.

In 1972 five skeletons of the dinosaur *Oviraptor* ("egg thief") were found in Mongolia. Not only did these *Oviraptors* have collarbones—they had *connected* left and right collarbones, very much like a bird's furcula. This discovery also seemed to support Huxley's ideas.

Oviraptor

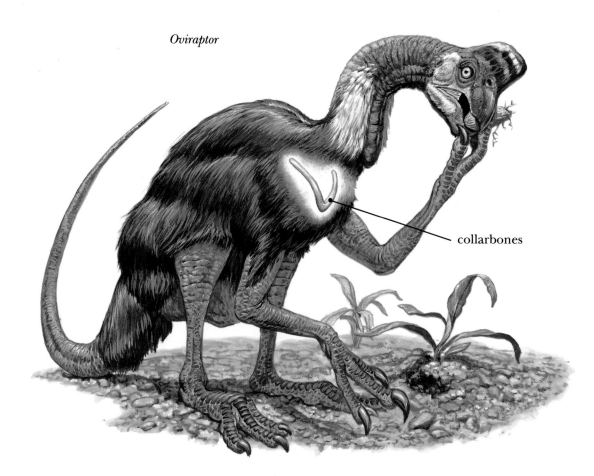

collarbones

In the 1700s Swedish scientist Carolus Linnaeus invented a system of organizing information about living things. It is called "classification." It places living things in different classes, or groups, according to features they have in common. Birds are in the class called Aves, mammals are in the class Mammalia, and reptiles—including dinosaurs—are in the class Reptilia.

Mammalia
(Mammals)

Reptilia
(Reptiles)

Aves
(Birds)

When *Archaeopteryx* was discovered, Thomas Huxley was so excited by the dinosaur-bird connection that he thought these classes should be changed. He wanted to put birds and reptiles—including dinosaurs—together in a new class, and call it "Sauropsida." Not many scientists agreed.

Recently, paleontologist Robert Bakker has come up with another idea. Dinosaurs, he says, were very special—different from other reptiles in many ways, and more like birds in a lot of ways. Bakker believes we should take dinosaurs out of the class Reptilia, and instead put dinosaurs and birds together in a class called "Dinosauria."

Again, most scientists do not agree. So in spite of the close dinosaur-bird connection, dinosaurs are still classed with reptiles, not with birds.

You Be the Scientist

Suppose you were a scientist back when *Archaeopteryx* was discovered. What would you have decided? Was it a bird? Or a dinosaur?

Think about all the things you know about it. How was it more like a bird? How was it more like a dinosaur? You might want to organize your facts in a chart, possibly like this:

	Feathers	*Tailbone*
Dinosaurs	No	Long
Archaeopteryx	Yes	Long
Today's Birds	Yes	Stumpy

Other features to consider could be teeth, claws, feet, and skeletons. Which had the most things in common—dinosaurs and *Archaeopteryx*? Or today's birds and *Archaeopteryx*? How do you rate the importance of these different features?

How about classification? Do you think Bakker's idea is a good one? Would you say that dinosaurs have more in common with birds, and less in common with other reptiles? Or do you agree with Huxley that birds, dinosaurs, and other reptiles should all be classed together? Maybe you have your own idea about how dinosaurs should be classified.

Present system:	*class Aves* Birds	*class Reptilia* Dinosaurs plus other reptiles
Huxley's idea:	*new class Sauropsida* Birds Dinosaurs plus other reptiles	
Bakker's idea:	*class Reptilia* All reptiles except dinosaurs	*new class Dinosauria* Birds Dinosaurs

What about the name? Do you think *Archaeopteryx* is the greatest name anyone could have picked? What would you have named it?

Scientific names are based on Latin and Greek. Here are some words and syllables you might want to use:

pteron = wing or feather

archaeo = ancient   *avis* = bird

deinos = terrible   *saurus* = reptile

animale = animal   *Germanus* = German

How about "Archaeoavis" (ancient bird)? Or "Avissaurus" (bird-reptile)? Or "Sauroavis" (reptile-bird)?

Maybe you have some better ideas.

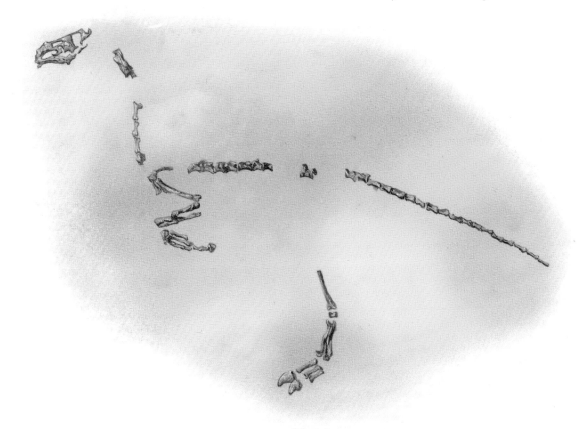

An Ancient Bird in Texas?

In 1983 a strange discovery was made in Texas. At first paleontologist Sankar Chatterjee thought he had found the remains of two baby dinosaurs. Then, as he worked on the skeletons, putting them together piece by piece, he suspected that he had something even more exciting. Soon he was convinced that these were not dinosaurs, but birds—birds that had lived 225 million years ago. That is 75 million years before *Archaeopteryx*!

In some ways they seemed more birdlike than *Archaeopteryx*. According to Dr. Chatterjee, they had fewer teeth. (Today's birds are toothless.) They seemed to have a heavy breastbone, a modern bird feature that *Archaeopteryx lithographica* did not have. And they may have had a more modern-shaped furcula than *Archaeopteryx*.

33

Dr. Chatterjee named his find *Protoavis texensis* ("first bird from Texas"). There was one big problem with *Protoavis*. There was no sign of feathers. So—was it really a bird, or not? Dr. Chatterjee says yes. He claims there are indirect signs of feathers—little bumps along the arm bones where the feathers were attached.

Other experts examined *Protoavis*. Nicholas Hotton III of the Smithsonian Institution said, "It looks 'bird.' It's difficult to see how it could be anything else."

What *Protoavis texensis* might have looked like

John Ostrom also examined it, and he has strong doubts. He says the bones were so broken up and crushed that he could not see bumps or any other sign that there had been feathers attached. He also does not think there was a furcula. As of 1995, Sankar Chatterjee could not show enough evidence to convince Ostrom and others that *Protoavis* was really a bird.

Sinornis

Other Early Birds

In 1987 another "early bird" was found, this one in China. It was named *Sinornis* ("Chinese bird"). *Sinornis* was no bigger than a sparrow. It lived 135 million years ago, about 15 million years after *Archaeopteryx*. Like *Archaeopteryx*, it had teeth. But in other ways it was more birdlike. The body and tailbone were shorter, and its wings were more winglike. No doubt about it: *Sinornis* was a good flyer.

In 1994 *Confuciusornis sanctus* ("holy Confucius bird") was discovered, also in China. Some scientists think this bird may have lived close in time to *Archaeopteryx*, although that is very uncertain. And not only did it have no teeth—it had a birdlike beak! Like *Sinornis,* it is one more link in the story of how birds got to be birds.

A New Discovery

In 1992 a new *Archaeopteryx* discovery was made. This brought the total number of specimens to seven. This last one was different from all the others. It *did* have a heavy breastbone, which means it probably was a stronger flyer.

It is considered to be a separate species of *Archaeopteryx* and has been named *Archaeopteryx bavarica*. This fossil is still being studied.

Parts of the puzzle of the dinosaur-bird connection may never be solved. We do keep making new discoveries. With each discovery we learn more. But it is likely that some parts of the mystery will lie buried forever.

Some scientists now go so far as to say that birds are "flying dinosaurs." This may be stretching the facts. As John Ostrom has said, "I prefer not to think of your canary as a dinosaur, or *Tyrannosaurus* as a bird."

Still, the next time you see a pigeon, a robin, a blue jay, or any other kind of bird, it can be a reminder that dinosaurs are not totally gone… because some part of them lives on in the birds of today.

Archaeopteryx Discoveries So Far

1861. Discovery of two-inch-long feather.

1861 (about a month later). Discovery of first feathery skeleton. Given the name *Archaeopteryx lithographica*.

1877. A more complete skeleton found, including skull.

1956. Badly preserved skeleton found in quarry shed by student.

1970. Wrongly identified "pterosaur" correctly identified by John Ostrom. (Specimen actually discovered back in 1855.)

1973. Another fossil correctly identified. (Specimen actually found in 1951, but first thought to be chicken-sized dinosaur *Compsognathus*.)

1987. One more skeleton found. It too was first misidentified as *Compsognathus*.

1992. New *Archaeopteryx* discovery, different because of its heavy breastbone. It is considered a separate species and has been named *Archaeopteryx bavarica*.

All of these were found in limestone quarries in Germany. In 1984 some *Archaeopteryx*-like bones were found in Romania. It is still not certain whether they belong to an *Archaeopteryx*. If they do, it will be the first to be found in a different location.

Bibliography

ANDERSON, ALUN. "Early Bird Threatens *Archaeopteryx*'s Perch." *Science,* Vol. 253, July 5, 1991.

BAKKER, ROBERT T. *The Dinosaur Heresies.* New York: Morrow, 1986.

BEARDSLEY, TIM. "Fossil bird shakes evolutionary hypotheses." *Nature,* Vol. 322, August 21, 1986.

BROWNE, MALCOLM W. "Two Clues Back Idea That Birds Arose From Dinosaurs." *The New York Times,* December 28, 1993.

CHARIG, ALAN. *A New Look at the Dinosaurs.* New York: Facts on File, Inc., 1983.

CHATTERJEE, SANKAR. "Skull of *Protoavis* and Early Evolution of Birds." *Journal of Vertebrate Paleontology,* September 16, 1987.

COLBERT, EDWIN H. *Evolution of the Vertebrates,* 3rd ed. New York: Wiley, 1980.

GOULD, STEPHEN JAY. "The Archaeopteryx Flap." *Natural History,* Vol. 95, September, 1986.

———. "The Telltale Wishbone." *Natural History,* Vol. 86, November, 1977.

LAMBERT, DAVID (The Diagram Group). *The Dinosaur Data Book.* New York: Avon, 1990.

———. *A Field Guide to Dinosaurs.* New York: Avon, 1983.

NORMAN, DAVID. *The Illustrated Encyclopedia of Dinosaurs.* New York: Crescent Books, 1985.

OSTROM, JOHN H. "A New Look at Dinosaurs." *National Geographic,* Vol. 154, No. 2. August, 1978.

———. "The bird in the bush." *Nature,* Vol. 353, September 19, 1991.

PAUL, GREGORY S. *Predatory Dinosaurs of the World.* New York: Simon and Schuster/A New York Academy of Sciences book, 1988.

SERENO, PAUL C., AND RAO CHENGGANG. "Early Evolution of Avian Flight and Perching: New Evidence from the Lower Cretaceous of China." *Science,* February 14, 1992.

WALLACE, JOSEPH. *The Rise and Fall of the Dinosaur.* New York: Gallery Books, 1987.

WILFORD, JOHN NOBLE. "Texas Fossil May Be Birds' Oldest Ancestor." *The New York Times,* August 14, 1986.

Index and Pronunciation Guide
Boldface page numbers refer to illustrations